MUNDANE MIRACLES

IVAN JENSON

CITY STONE
PUBLISHING

CITY STONE PUBLISHING

ISBN: 978-1-915399-15-1 (paperback)
ISBN: 978-1-915399-16-8 (ePUB)

A CIP catalogue record for this book is available from the British Library.

Ivan Jenson | www.ivanjenson.com
City Stone Publishing | www.citystonepublishing.com

First printed: November 2022
Second edition: March 2023

CONTENTS

LAST CALL

Why didn't you
say this
when we were
both beautiful
I mean look at us now
our shoes are shinier
than our complexions
and when was the last time
we were complimented by
our own reflections
at this stage we would rather
sleep too damn much
than search the city at night
for a stranger selling
the soft drug called touch
anyway, you say
you still know your way
around a midnight mattress
and this time
I won't mix and match
my feelings
or misplace your
rusty red kiss

CHEATING MYSELF

When you gave me
that token of your
affection
I must confess
I used it to
take the subway
uptown
to meet up
with someone
who didn't
love me as much
because it's been taxing
with you always asking
how much I care
that's what's so great
about roaming
Wi-Fi reception
I can always tune in
to tireless, wireless
deception

Simple Subtraction

This is how we slowly
lose everything
either we misplace
a book or the memory
of a face or we
forget to call
for days and years
on end
or just maybe
we even forget
we were once
a baby
and then someone
has to remind us
to listen
to a complaint
or a compliment
and finally, we shed
thoughts of the dead
and no longer smile
when we think
of a toast
that was made
when former friends
were wed
and just when
we think
we have found happiness
it turns out to be
all in our head

Momentary Lapse

The sunshine
was the perfect
storm of light
and its rays
were like breakfast
in bed served
on reflecting
silver trays
and her shoulder
as she turned away
was any photographer's
dream shot
and the afternoon
waited to arrive
like a tourist wearing
loud shorts
on their way
to the Florida Keys
anyway, that was
the morning he
never asked
her not to leave him
pretty please

BLOGGED DOWN

I have my own theories
about the hyperbole
of your hypothesis
and I really want to lose
your findings
mostly because
you go for that
which is photorealist
while I am more
the abstract expressionist
drunk on shots of my own ego
I am the chain-smoking addict
making history out of my own misery
while you are the disgruntled critic
you see, I just make it happen
no matter how kitsch
scratching the surface of
the insatiable cultural itch
I am the low blow
to your high-brow pastiche
and since you cannot do it
Discouragement 101
is the only course
you can teach

ROOM TEMPERATURE

When morning feels
more like evening
and wine tastes like water
then you know
something is thinning
like the hair of a
middle-aged man
and so, you walk in rain
on a sunny day
knowing that
there is a chill
to the end of summer
that hints at the fall
which always leads
to winter's grip
when you know
that all you do
like your footsteps
in the snow
will melt like streams
leading to rivers
and finally, to the ocean
you see, everything
is as it seems
during this emotion
and it is getting late
almost time to go
home on the range
under the acid rain
this is your own personal
climate change

ALREADY SAVED

I sped past
a billboard
which stated in big bold letters exactly
what I should do
and I still could not take
that highway advice
mostly because
I don't believe Jesus
has an 800 number
and I'd rather leave
certain things
in a state of perpetual wonder
so I drove to your place
where you greeted me
with a forced smile
and your freshly washed hair
and that is when I felt
a tinge of jealousy
because I was sure
you weren't alone
and God was there

THEM AGAIN

Usually, they arrive
fifteen minutes
to half an hour late
though some
come on time
they often bring
dishes to pass
or kisses to the
cheek
they often kick
the snow off
their boots
then compliment you
on your decor
or bore you
with the
hard time
they had
getting to you
because of some
pile up on the highway
or some minor
emergency with
their spouse, kid,
mother or boss

then they will toss
their down jacket
on the bed
where all the coats
are stacked
and then you will
spend an evening
talking, eating, laughing,
drinking, sitting, standing,
dancing, eyes darting
from person to person
searching for someone
to fill the void
you were trying to avoid
by inviting them
to fill the never-ending
empty cup
that you call
home

MEET AND GREET

What would
your average
everyday
shrink
think
about that time
you thought your
cell was lost
or stolen
and how you
called yourself
from your landline
and the relief
you felt when
you heard it vibrate
under your Chihuahua
so you picked
it up and
said "Hi"
to yourself
for the first time

CARE PACKAGE

I don't have
a woman
who is my rock
and behind this
good man is nothing
but thin dead air
and my only encouragements
are the rare moments
when I snap myself
or slap myself
out of discouragement
and yet they say she will
happen when I least
expect it
like a bill
for a benign biopsy
in the mail
that I thought my
insurance would cover
and at last, I will gasp
at the emotional cost
I will pay
when the universe
sends me my
Medicaid lover

GOOD FOR YOU

The sad truth about
happiness
is that it does not tell
the whole story
there is no follow-up
to see if the recipient
has maintained their
quota of endorphins
or whether the butterflies
in their stomach have
flown out their mouths
as they sleep off
that night of a thousand stars
a couple of dive bars
some french fries
and french kissing in
convertible cars...
What about the following
Monday morning
when they
clock in at the factory
that manufactures
the assembly line of days
the nuts and bolts
and occasional
electric jolts
of broken heart parts
who is there
with the questionnaire
to learn
their long-term
status quo
and check if they
still have joy
yes or no?

WALLPAPER

You share
snippets
of snapshots
which create
a dream-collage
of torn-off truths
and made-up
black and white
manifestations of
what might have been
and on that
bulletin board
riddled with
thumbtack facts
scotch-taped
with sticky situations
that you emotionally
detached
from your store-bought
Hallmark Heart
I see
the calendar
in your room
reveals
all you have
to look forward to
is a Zumba class
at noon

HUMAN RACE

One day you are
going to cough up
a cacophony
of camouflaged
fuselage
funnelled through
the filter of
your native tongue
and this siphoned
fuel to the fire
will fill up the tanks
of a thousand
rumbling motors
parallel parked
in the empty lot
filled with
those driven
to the brink of
diesel despair
but when they
hear your
hallowed honk
they will all
swerve to the curve
because you
had the nerve
to speed in place
like a Buddha mobile
at the Indy 500

SWAN SONG

When it's time for me
to play my hand
let loose the tigers
set off the pyrotechnics
signal the band
and sing my last number
the one that will bring
down the house
and when I am as spent
as Elvis doing
a karate chop on stage
then allow me to
bow out and burn out
my way
like Howard Hughes
hitchhiking on the highway
who only wishes for more
minutes not millions
to spend
before the end

Matrix Complex

I wasn't there
during the
pinnacle points
in history
and I am barely
here now when nothing
in particular happens
but I do plan to attend
the beginning of the end
of all my struggles and strife
and when I have the form
of happiness commonly
known as love
I will privately step
outside to thank
the teenage aliens playing
the reality simulator above

SOUL SEARCH

If I don't see tangible
results within the
foreseeable future
then I am going to
have to reach into
my past to locate
and point a finger at
a formidable figure
or figurine that is
to blame
for making me
into the damaged goods
that I am
and when I pinpoint
that moment
when I pivoted
or pirouetted
in the wrong direction
I will say "ah ha!"
and patch up that
gaping hole
in the holistic
hologram of my
humanity
and then I will
go get
me
some
sushi

SORRY INDIVIDUAL

As a novelist
I apologize for
lifting our
conversations
verbatim and
strategically
placing them in
quicksilver plots
spoken by
sunny
or shady
characters
as a poet
forgive me
for making you
naked to
the world
of deep navel
gazing divers

and as
a painter
excuse me
for exhibiting
your full frontal
frailties
in the gallery
of public
opinion
and as
a man
I ask that
you see
me only
as that spark
in the dark
which is
my only
true art

FLOWERY LANGUAGE

Tonight
we get
numerological
astrological
far flung
and farfetched
and we will
believe in
old and young
wives tales
and we will
speak in
the french tongues
of channelers
who channel
surf the
cosmetic
cosmos
of each other's
complexion
tomorrow
we will
come to
our senseless
sentimental
selves
and
beg
each other's
pardon
yet forever
promise
a rose garden

ME AND THE MRS.

Waves of expression
wash across your face
the wind brushes your hair
the mist glosses your smile
and the backdrop seascape
competes for
the casual cinematographer
of my gaze
and yet I neither
propose marriage nor a toast
or in a seductive inflection
test your boundaries
with an indiscreet suggestion
instead, I seize this stolen moment
so that it will last my whole life
and I take a selfie with you
though you remain
someone else's wife

ACQUAINTANCE FORGOTTEN

I am piecing together
a string of thoughts
made of featherweight
implications and
free-floating flattery
which flutter like
your eyelashes
or the flicker
of the outdoor
candlelight
and it occurs
to me that nothing
significant
has occurred
which would
call for rejoicing or
a celebratory
urban tribal dance
to eighties' music
and there is nothing
here to remember
cherish or regret
we simply chatted
and learned we have
only liquor, August
and evening
mosquito bites
in common
and tonight
we certainy
won't
scratch
each other's
itch   22

Trick of the Trade

You reappeared
like a magician's
lovely assistant
and it turned out
our relationship
had not been
sawed in two
as I had feared
instead, it remained
perfectly intact
and then when our love
like a dove
flew out from your hat
I knew your kiss
had cast a spell
and you were
one gifted illusionist

MIMING MY OWN BUSINESS

I am
sent
like a
clown
to sculpt
the colorful
helium
balloons
of language
and when my
squeaky
masterpieces
are done
they lift off
into the sky
like mini-Snoopys
so please
don't rain
on my
Thanksgiving
parade
just
consider me
a Jack-in-the-Box
of all
trades
and
a master
of pun

REFILL PICK UP

I would have
to put on
my reading glasses
to make out the fine print
written in your gaze
in response
to my feeble attempt
to bring a smile
to your face
but I don't want to
have to research
your chemical reaction
I always knew
that the medicinal
effect of your affection
came with a list
of side effects
that could have
scared me away
yet I trust my
Walgreens woman
and the FDA

GHOST WRITER

You are displaying
a total lack of artistry
when you fail to
edit your anger
or revise that look
in your eyes
and that raw
manuscript of
gripes and grievances
you tossed 'cross my desk
still doesn't make
me love you any less
because you could write
a trilogy about how much
you despise me
and I would still
pore over your pages
punctuated with rages
because you see
the burning book
I have taken off the shelf
is the autobiography
I wrote about myself

THE SCHEME OF THINGS

Listen, it is all
written in stone
by Shakespeare Michelangelo
and even your expletives
are eloquent poetry
composed by kids on candy
your movements
a modern dance
of ancient ritual
your conquests pitiful
your failures grandiose
as a grand piano
in the Grand Canyon
played by a granny
with a Grammy
so the next time
opportunity knocks
on your knucklehead
get the heck out of bed
and smell the coffee
because besides
living fully
is there something else
pending you have to do
instead?

PRE-POSTHUMOUS

What will they say
about me
while I am still alive
and kicking
cans down the road
and while blood pulses
through that which
I do in vain?
Will I wind up
crazy for all
that is sane
like a sack of potatoes
weighing down
a gravy train?
And will they honour
my valiant effort
while I am still a human
able to sign and sign
an authograph
on the shoulder
of a beautiful woman?
Or will I have to wait
to be discovered
like the tomb of
Tutankhamun?

YES REGRETS

I press rewind
in my mind
and replay
favorite days
some of them quite
insignificant
yet they resonate
and sometimes I wish
I could tap the shoulder
of the former me
and tell him not
to make certain choices
at other times
I just sit back
and listen to
youthful or
ancient voices
and look in wonder
at the tribal dance
of past romance
in any case
if I had the chance
to do it all over again
I would ask for more
of love's
flammable
extinguishable
exquisite pain

NEIGHBORHOOD WATCH

I didn't come here
to confront you
or to pledge
undying love
nor am I part
of an intervention
to save you
from yourself
and I am not
bearing gifts
or cash
to buy you out
of a deal
or to keep
your lips sealed
and I know
I came unannounced
not because a check
has bounced
or to be the bearer
of bad news
and I don't stand
before you
to promote
a candidate
or to get
a date
I am here
just to see
my reflection
in your eyes
to remind myself
that I am still
alive

PRIZED POSSESSION

I am standing
imperfectly still
waiting for
whoever just
broke into my
consciousness
to take what they
want and get out
without harming me
but sure enough
they find my
hiding place
steal a kiss
as well as
my most expensive
work of art
a highly breakable heart

BLESS ME

I fully expect
a surprise party
when I walk
in the door
or to bump into
the love of
my next life
while minding
my current affairs
so instead of
acting like this
is a dress rehearsal
I treat every moment
like anything can happen
and though usually
nothing does
it's worth noting
that even Mona Lisa smiles
just because

MANSPLAINING

I can't believe it
has all been spent
the evenings with
pink champagne friends
and midnight snacks
with temp lovers dressed
in my down comforters
and happy and unhappy
New Year's Eves
making highly breakable
resolutions
and even the wasted
afternoons seem as precious
as farewell airport kisses
or a good laugh with
a friend while doing dishes
and I guess like cash
I don't know how to
hold on to a moment's notice
and now I'm so sorry
I scolded you for being late
when it was a blessing
that you showed up at all
even though you are
now just a framed photo
on my wall
I am ready to
admit what most won't
people are made up of
now you see love
now you don't

PARTY OF ONE

I suppose it's fine
that only a little wine
spilled on my vest
making me look like
a wounded guest
and I am perfectly OK
keeping my thoughts
to myself
exploring the books
on the shelf
sure, I hoped I would blend
and my loneliness would end
at least the dip was spicy
and the music was decent
and even if the one joke
I told fell flat
because it was possibly
politically incorrect
at least I put myself out there
and that is commendable
I deserve a medal of honour
for reaching out socially
even if staying home
and watching Netflix
would have made me
less miserable

MUNDANE MIRACLES

I saw a silent husband
walking with a talkie wife
in the black and white night
and through a bedroom window
a significant other
watched TV
with her Technicolor lover
as a feral cat perused
which proved
no place is better than home
under the cinematic dome
of stars hovering over
dark parked cars
and moonlit picket fences
stripping my defenses
as I walk this dog of mine
for the umpteenth time
and none of it registered
as anything more
than commonplace
though you wouldn't know it
by the look of wonder
that nobody saw
upon my face

Made in the Shade

I am sorry
that I had to turn
and go back
when you were
leading me
towards the light
it's just that I forgot
my sunglasses
and the UV
of that destination
was beyond my
personal vision
I guess I can't
stare directly into
the rays of
spirituality
as a person
who wasn't
born yesterday
to be born again
at this point
would be just a bit
too much for me

ROADKILL

I was never
personally introduced
to myself
instead, I got to
know my likes
and dislikes
like a hit and miss
game of tennis
with my alter ego
which happened
to be a pro
at under and over-handed
insults and compliments
and now that I understand
the underlying motives
behind much of what
I say and do
I can see that
despite my wrongs
and my rights
I am really just a
deer in the headlights

A Decent Proposal

Come with me
on a far from
breath-taking
adventure
for a lifetime
which will consist
of little victories
and faint fanfare
from a few friends
and our only travels
will be from the fluorescent
shores of Walmart
over a few speedbumps
to join forces
with the frugal soldiers
of the Salvation Army
who like us,
are bargain hunters
even though
the only
battle I will
fight for you
will be
from my
beer-bellied bulge

and the only
protection I can
provide will be
the bark
of our small dog
dear
let's hide together
here
in my suburban
submarine which
each
day sinks
like my heart
if you don't take
me up
on my cheapskate
chivalry

REPURPOSED

I am wearing her ex's
bathrobe and slippers
'cause I got caught
in a sudden downpour
meanwhile my Levi identity
and my Fruit of the Loom
elastic dreams
and V-Neck what the heck
sock-it-to-me
way of getting by
is tumbling in the dryer
as I sip hot cocoa
by a fire
and I would do it all again
because nothing can keep me away
from this divorcee
certainly not
a little rain

Happy Trending

There is no
coach rooting me on
or father sitting in the wings
not even a paper bag lunch
made by mother
and my shirt was not
starched and ironed by a lover
there is no fan club
begging for my signature
or an audience member
being ushered to their
seat by an usher
and a journalist
didn't just ask
how it feels
to be me
and you probably
don't even know
who I am
and yet despite
my lack of subscribers
or financial advisers
I am still my biggest fan

NEED A RIDE?

You must know that
everything
you cling to
is just a promise made
of tap-dancing water
like a black-tie event
followed by
the migraine of rain
and even the honeymoon
of sun worship
ends in a roll
of the dry ice
which keeps you shivering
in the middle of a Nor'easter
with your pants falling down
because you forgot
to tighten your bible belt
it's best to take
pretty crinkled noses
at face value
and when one
offers you a free ride
to where you already are
get in the damn car

Scrolling through the Years

You are looking good
and doing well
at juggling two
polar opposite
mental states
as well as a son
and a dropped dream
of being Jennifer Aniston
at least you keep
everything in the air
including your
salt and pepper hair
up in a bun
it's amazing how much
you look like each other
I'm not talking about your kid
but rather the you
I once affectionately called "hun"
anyway, it made me smile
when I accidentally on purpose
happened upon
your Facebook profile

A Roast of a Toast

I am standing up in
ovation
for all those
who have been
knighted by
the evening light,
with wine in hand
they glow and gloat
and lay out their
best laid plans
which come to
fruition
since they
can afford
the tuition
to the Ivy league
of ladies
and gentleman
callers
ahead for
reservations
to four-course
seasons of
seasoned
sensations

and they are
always seated
front row and
center for
the theater
of the superb
and though
the cream
of the American
dream, rises
to the top
someday,
even
the gravy train
has to come
to a halt
and we all
gotta do
the mashed potato

STAR-SPANGLED

I am
a half-mast flag,
flapping in the wind
representing a fraction
of my country
having spent over
half a century
undocumented
by historians
living out the improv
of my destiny
and one day they will say
that I am survived
by the blinking and breathing
who will cough and cry
at the monotony
of my eulogy
and what remains
of my karmic debt
will be repaid
where my best
plans will finally
be laid down
in the anti-climax
of my nakedness
don't worry
only worms
and angels
will know what
to make of this

Color Blind

I was tickled pink
by your code red
warning that I
might end up
black and blue
should I choose
not to white out
what had me
blue in the face
and so, I acknowledged
my gray areas
which I could not see
amidst the purple prose
then I drank
the orange juice
of inspiration
and saw with
my own two eyes
the psychedelic rainbow
of a new morning sunrise

ADULT BEVERAGE

When you offered your hand
like an olive branch
I felt peace for the first time
in this war-torn heart
then when the wind
carried a message of warning
I knew I might return
to waking up alone
in the morning
yet when I considered
the odds of my being born
and of us having kissed
I knew that there was
something in the equation
that I missed
I guess love is tart
and there's an art
to drinking the martini
mixed with you and me
and a twist

CUP HALF-FULL

To seek and to never
find and to wish
without becoming
fulfilled and then
to ask and to be denied
by the powers that be
to look and to never
recognize what
is plain to see
like ignorant bliss
with a college degree
then to try to
exit the entry door
is to know how
my ancestors' lost
cause must have felt
like a terminal patient
walking against
an airport
conveyer belt
in any case
I think you get
what I mean
this is how it feels
before I've had
my morning caffeine

A Leg Up

As an individual who
lives
within
a public persona
as a shower
soul singer
trapped
in the body
of a bad
dancer
as a spokesman
for a generation
that has already
spoken for
itself
as an elder statesman
who still harbors
juvenile
justifications for the
unjust
gesticulations
of gentile
gentrification
which only
generates
a higher cost

for general
admission
to this movie
theater
I want you to know
I acknowledge your
right to taunt
the hell out of me
by putting your feet
up on the seat
next to mine
but allow you this
impolite
indiscretion
due to
your
gender
selection
and the
pink polish
on your
ten
tenacious toes

LESSON LEARNED

So much is
revealed
as I unravel
and many of the pieces
may never fit
who says the cheekbones
of time
must be symmetrical
it's OK
if my questions
to the universe
are rhetorical
there is a point
when even mentors
throw up their hands
like the time I ran into
a private teacher
in a public space
and knew by the quizzical
look on his face
that he was not
a know-it-all
but rather just someone
I bumped into
at the mall

HIRE-ABILITY

Allow me to approach
this evening like
a holiday party,
business casual
I will bring something
to the table
and if necessary, I will
roll up my sleeves and
dance wacky
in my khakis
I will drink too much
spiked punch
and make a fool
of myself and
almost get punched
making my co-workers
talk under their breath
and then I will go home
with the boss' daughter
and get fired
the morning after
all because my true job
has always been
to make sure my life
is something I enjoyed
even if I am now
utterly unemployed

TARGET AUDIENCE

I want to write something
that will be translated
into at least
twenty languages
or create a product
that will be shipped
worldwide
or maybe paint
a picture that
will be put in a
bulletproof frame
and periodically restored
by gentle experts in white gloves
 but I guess I must accept
that the most I will ever achieve
is to maybe do a little something
that someone like you loves

HOOK-UP

It's official
this whole
thing is superficial
and based solely
on mutual distraction
from emotional depth
or even worse
spiritual meaning
because sometimes
it's fun to downgrade
expectations and indulge
in soft-core
consensual conversation
consisting of
non-intellectual innuendo
and zero love
so tomorrow
don't even wait
for my text
instead, when you
think of me
just whisper the word
"next"

GONE WOMAN

I will now make sure
to water
the front lawn
of the house
you left behind
and I will try to keep
the flowers in bloom
as well as make sure
to sweep empty rooms
with the lonely broom
including the dust
in the one that
became your
make-shift tomb...
I have set up my
office there
where I compose
my minor key thoughts
like silent symphonies
he sort that fall
on deaf ears
I bet you're drinking
on a cloud
with Beethoven or Mozart
as I attempt to turn
average everyday sorrow
into post-modern
post-mother art

THE DOT CON

I thought that you
were seeking a self-starter
an independent thinker
a free spirit who had a
sixth sense of the marketplace
who could anticipate
what hungry young professionals
and the gentrified generation
wanted when they switched
on and plugged in their
up-to-the-minute
Google gadgets
but now I see you just wanted
me to affirm this company's
right to shove your
sugar substitute
for quality, meaning and love
down the online throats
of consumers
and so, I resign
Lord,
deliver me
from this
silicon
valley of
despair
to the pearly
Bill Gates of
Heaven

ROOMMATES AND LOVERS

Like the way
you always say "like"
as if nothing is
any more real
than a movie
and how you
move me
from room to room
following your moods
and chasing your future
as if we could ever get past
the cursing moments written
in cursive sound waves mid-air
before you flipped your hair
flippantly as if you
could care less
and were probably
just bored
anyway, this is
the only love
life we can afford

FUN IN THE SUN

You hide your
true personality
in plain sight
and so, when I get
to your core
you pretend to snore
as if you were only
dreaming this
near-life
experience
I think
a pop psychologist
would have a field day
uncorking
your champagne pain
What I am saying
is that you're all wet
if you think you need
to always be the best
stop clinging
to the idea
that your life
is a wet T-shirt contest

VIRAL PHENOMENA

I want you all
to get up and out of
your seats and
put your hands together
for the latest sensation
on social media
so that you can
worship their wardrobe
and envy their lifestyle
then watch as they
make a wrong move
or release an inferior
product which crashes
and burns their
career and personal life
then I want you
to celebrate their
inevitable comeback
and accept their
new fuller figure
and entitled offspring
now watch as they
suffer personal tragedy
substance abuse
and see them
burst into
the flames of
inflammatory
controversy

now witness
their televised
and puffy-eyed
appearances
in the court
of public
disapproval
then watch
them become
truly immortal
by having
the gall to die
now watch
and listen
to their eulogy
on your TVs, phones
and devices
then click on
the next
hot new thing
trending
and don't forget
to share

HOW IT'S DONE

You start out
a beginner
work your way
to intermediate
and advance
to advanced
until you find
you have gone
from rookie
to master
and now
you discover
yourself
to be
a youngish,
elder statesman
and the next
generation
of newbies
look to you
for inspiration
and advice
on how to
skip a few
steps in the
long
drawn-out
process
of making it
to the top
and you hate
to break it to them
but it all starts
at the bottom
with a mop

Unadulterated Facts

I am discontinuing
my subscription
to the periodic
delivery of glossy
fleshy fantasy
and I am instead
facing full frontal
reality
cellulite and all
and I am no longer
photo shopping
around for
doctored
perfection
instead
I am accepting
the crow's feet
of nature
and the slow
sag of time
and I hope
you too will
accept my
body
mass
index
and love me
like
good
cholesterol

DATE

I knew a stranger
intimately
and we behaved
as though we had
known each other
several lifetimes
we finished the other's
sentences and laughed
prior to punchlines
while sharing the same
glass of wine
one of us leaving
lipstick stains
and we played
a game of strip poker
without a deck of cards
then she called an Uber
and gathered up
her things and her
composure
it was then I knew
I would never get
closure

JADED JOURNEY

I move
through a dusty
cluttered room
to a paint-peeled door
that leads to a driveway
with weeds
punching through
where I get in
my old jalopy Ford
with its tattered seats
and start the elderly engine
which clears its metallic throat
and then I drive aimlessly
through the rain
on an errant errand
and distracted
by the rubbish
of redundancy
I briefly forget
that my to-do list
will one day
be all checked off
and come to
a bitter end

WILD CHILD

You try to understand
where they are coming from
after they come home
at five a.m. inebriated
you try to see things
their way
as they stare blankly
at the walls
you try to truly hear
what they are saying
as they mumble indecipherably
under their breath like Brando
and you think you can save them
but then they dive into the deep end
of a pool filled
with empty sorrow
and so, you try
to resuscitate them
with your kiss of life
but like a stray black cat
that has brought you bad luck
they know damn well
they have at least
nine lives left
so they don't mind
wasting your only one

ONE-PERCENTER

Let me decide
for myself
if success is as empty
as they say
and I will let you know
if dating a Swedish model
in the French Riviera
is vapid and will
rapidly lead to
my soul's decay
and when my
pretty bank teller
sees my current balance
and her pupils start dilating
don't tell me this
won't feel like
a spiritual awakening
because I have been
chasing that star-studded
gold-leafed, sugar-coated,
gift-wrapped jackpot
since I was old enough
to watch
the Beverly Hillbillies
on TV
so don't you even try
to stop me from
sipping on some
good ol' Texas tea

LONESOME DOVE

I don't share
my life with
one particular
person in the
traditional sense
instead, I have built
an amazingly effective
invisible fence
that keeps my dogged
pride from running away
from this private property
and possibly getting run over
and once in a great while
I let in the unexpected
visitor who happens
to be in the area
and just thought
they'd stop on by
and we have
cookies and coffee
and when they leave
I wave goodbye
as their car
pulls out of the drive
while holding my
caged heart
yet it somehow
escapes like
a parakeet
into the skies
and that's when
I remember that
time flies

SPRING CLEANING

I still saved
everything you
gave me
and I have
stored all that
nothingness
in an empty room
in the attic of
my consciousness
next to undeveloped
negatives of what
could have been
positive
if only you
could have lived up
to the hype
of being
what I wanted
so much
but can now
live without
I guess
that is what
dandruff and dust
are all about

Legal Jargon

Always
copyright your life
story
so that nobody
steals your unique
plot
better yet
dictate your
autobiography
to a dedicated
biographer
some in-house
stenographer
who has the infinite
patience to transcribe
the intimate first person
subjective narrative
that you describe
in painstaking
lovemaking
detail

and make sure not
to gloss over
every he-said she-said
moment that
made your epic
journey so special
this way you
can always sue
anybody
who tries to
infringe on
the fringe benefit
of having the patent
on being the one
and only
insufferable
you

LOW PROFILE

There is a lot
I could, should,
or would do
if I was brave
and bold
and outgoing
like cliff or
social climbers
but I tend to stick
close to home-base
rather than step outside
and chase
elusive opportunities
disguised as
attainable goals
most nights I stay in
and count wolves
in sheep's clothing
and I never cease
to be amazed that
all my ambition
amounts to nothing more
than pillow fluffing

FLIPSIDE

By day
I am that guy
who you assume
is alright because
he is gregarious
and seems like
he really could
care less
and by night
I am the
phantom gentleman
who carries himself
like a Casanova castaway
who kissed the world
and made it cry
sadly smiling
with an overbite
on a defunct
online dating site
a lonely non-smoker
who often asks
the darkness
if it would
like a light

THE BIG COMEBACK

I was
once beautiful
respected far and wide
the toast of the town
considered the next big thing
expected to stay on top
traveled first class
pursued by women and the press
mentioned in the tabloids
paid handsomely
young as roses in bloom
whispered about in certain circles
the life of parties uptown and down
loved to the moon and back
dressed in Versace
with both parents alive and proud
now I'm
living in a modest home
walking like a zombie at a local mall
disappearing into a crowd
learning old friends have become somebody
driving while listening to 80s music
lost in fantasy at the pharmacy
a has-been who would-be if could-be
and yet just offered a major new contract
given a new lease on hope
checking with a lawyer if this is
too-good-to-be-true
assured this is a legitimate opportunity
pinching myself to make sure it isn't a dream
not even worried if this time it will or will not last
just ready to once again kick fame and fortune's ass

CONFESSIONS OF A NEW YORK CITY STREET ARTIST

I have stood with a homeless family
under a canopy on Fifth Avenue
during a downpour
all my paintings on a rolling cart
in the thick air of August
with two bucks in my pocket
I felt alive
I sold a painting to a man just released from prison
I sold to a couple who lived in a shelter with their child
I sold a work on paper for three dollars
and bought my girlfriend and me
hot dogs at Grey's Papaya on Broadway
she never looked happier
a wife of a plastic surgeon opened a briefcase
in her penthouse apartment dining room
on Columbus Circle containing eleven thousand cash
as payment for my six-foot canvas
I sold another work on paper to a lesbian Juilliard student
who kissed me on the lips as a thank you
I have sold in SoHo, Greenwich Village,
the Upper West Side, Fifth Avenue
Union Square, Sixth Avenue, and St. Mark's Place
I have snuck into street fairs in Little Italy and festivals
on Third Avenue
I sold a canvas on Cooper Square to a stripper
for two-hundred bucks, cash
I sold to a hunched old street jazz pianist
I have sold to cops and had my art confiscated by cops
I painted a large-scale portrait of a wealthy gay couple
for eight grand and the guys posed together naked
in my East Village storefront studio apartment

on a concrete city sidewalk,
I once made six hundred bucks in an hour
drawing pop art portraits of pedestrians on sketch pad paper
while getting high from inadvertently inhaling
the Pilot marker fumes
I have been commissioned to paint dogs, cats, and birds
I drew Jonathan Larson in a coffee shop on Avenue A
and he tried to convince me to do backdrops for
some sort of rock opera based on *La Bohème*
he was working on
and I was too stressed about my rent
to even consider it
I regret that to this day
I sold to the actor who played Angel in *Rent*
and the actress who later played Maureen in *Rent*
I videotaped her singing for me
and I told her she would one day be a star
and now she has won a Tony Award
and played Elsa in *Frozen*
and I have lost the video
I have sold in temperatures of one hundred degrees
I have sold on a New Year's Day in sub-zero weather
with a wind chill
I have made sales at midnight
in front of the now long-gone downtown Virgin megastore
I have said hello to almost every striking young woman
who happened to walk by
I would invite them to sit next to my set up
in a director's chair
beautiful Indian, Latin, or Scandinavian women
and NYU students
all sat and talked with me
I would treat them to Starbucks lattes

I was stood up by dozens of potential customers
as well as dozens of potential dates
I have been stood up on Saturday nights,
on the Fourth of July, and on Saint Patrick's Day
I have stood waiting for love in Washington Square,
the South Street Seaport, and Grand Central Station
an inebriated man once stumbled and
collapsed on my table of paintings
I have seen my art blown away by the wind
into the traffic on the Manhattan streets
I have lost paintings under parked trucks
kind strangers have chased my art
blowing down the sidewalk
one canvas caught a gust and just missed
striking an elderly woman in the head
I have discarded paintings only to have them
stolen from the trash outside my building
my painting of John Lennon was stabbed
in a club called Octagon
the millionaire owner reimbursed me
with only three hundred dollars
I was politely but briskly escorted
out of the office of Paloma Picasso
with my two giant rejected portraits of her
that barely fit in the elevator
I later sold one of those paintings for twelve grand cash
I have drawn millionaire and billionaire CEQs
on the Highlander Yacht of Malcolm Forbes
I painted his final portrait
I quoted a price, and he raised me five grand
in nightclubs I have drawn instant celebrity portraits
with markers on napkins
of Madonna, Mick Jagger, and Eddie Murphy

I have painted on a commission until nine a.m. in Ottawa, Canada
with ten-grand cash stuffed in my socks
my hotel had no safe
one day I arrived on a street and sold everything
for five hundred
and rolled my empty cart home to get more paintings
set up again and made five hundred more
I used to have a superstitious belief that if I saw a matinee
it wold bring me luck selling later on in the afternoon
and it did
I have sold my art in living room parties, disco boats,
bakeries, cafes,
The Palladium, Limelight, The World
and the Nirvana penthouse nightclub in Times Square
as well as at bars and an after-hours club called
Save the Robots
that didn't open until five a.m.
I have strapped paintings onto female jazz dancers
because the club owner
forbade me from displaying them on the walls
and so, I sold the paintings right off the dancers' backs
I have sold to gay men from Rome
rich trust-fund teenage girls from Beverly Hills
psychiatrists, physical therapists, Ric Ocasek from The Cars,
possible gangsters from Queens and Brooklyn
I have exchanged my art for dental work, podiatry,
and two round-trip tickets to Bermuda,
one round trick ticket to Rio,
and a round trip to Sweden to see a girl I loved
and she still broke my heart
when she didn't want to come back to New York with me
I have exchanged art for dinners at Benihana
I have been featured on Network News, Cable TV, and
Public Access channels

I have been chronically poor and periodically rich
I have seen my career reach peaks, where millionaires
proposed champagne toasts to my talent
on luxury yachts on the Hudson River
and I have stooped so low that I paced a psych ward
in soiled clothing
watching my whole life flash before me
like a movie montage
while I was too paranoid to even take a shower
I have painted and sold my art
for over thirty-five odd years
I have drawn or painted on boards, canvas, T-shirts,
and with my trusted jumbo Pilot marker
I have temporarily tattooed
the bare breasts, backs, shoulders, and thighs
of top models
I have a painted twenty-foot mural in a
high fashion showroom
and was known for painting on the backs of jeans jackets
or drawing on classroom chalk boards, sketch pads,
fine tablecloths of five Star Bistros,
and bald heads
I have drawn on the fog of taxicab windows
while looking out at my time zip by
and I have used cheap foam brushes and
expensive sable hairbrushes
and only a clinical depression and a psychotic break
halted my work
knocking me to the floor
but once I exorcised those inner demons
the art angels came back
to curse and bless me to continue
on my artistic journey
evermore

SUMMERING IN THE WINTE

I'm sorry
but I feel
like February
and you can't
convince me
to be more like June
and by the way
I am going to get
all Monday on you
if you don't keep
acting like
Friday night
when you know
damn well
this may be noon
but what you just
said so is midnight
and by that I don't
mean moonlight
and spirits
no I mean you
have turned
what was pure
nineties magic
and made it
year two thousand
and tragic

Hollywood Beginning

Maybe you will be
a friend of a friend
who shows up
in the nick of time
right at the end
before the credits roll
and we will
try to remember
each other's names
and where we
first met
and then I will ask
if you have time
for coffee or a drink
and you will say
"Sure, why not?"
And as if on cue
rain will fall
and we will share
an umbrella
and a few
shots later
it will be clear
this is our own rom com
and you are my gal
and I am your fella

THE MECHANIC

Here let me have a try
I know a little
about broken down people
sometimes all you have to do
is adjust their attitude
to get them on their feet again
most of the time
it can be done
by getting under their hood
and making them feel understood
there I just saved you thousands in therapy
and you don't even have to thank me
just remember to take it slow
and you should be good to go

INTERIOR DESIGN

I have painted myself
into a corner like
a typical artist
and created
a self-portrait
more somber
than an amber Rembrandt
all so that you can see me
framed by the captivity
of my creativity
a pigment of my
stagnant imagination
staring into open space
hung crooked on a nail
and I hope you
truly see
that I need you
to take the initiative
and straighten me

Temporary Remedy

Set these words
to music in your mind
and dance within your senses
as if you were intoxicated
on your wedding day
and everyone was there
to celebrate your love
now watch
what I write
become a living
breathing thing
like a firstborn
bundled up and crying
just for the sake of sound
and then I want you
to read carefully
the following directions:
take everything I say
for granted
and let this poem
disintegrate like
a prescribed tablet
on your tongue
and wait for the literary
ingredients
to flood your bloodstream
like an opioid
but be prepared
when you reach
the end of this
poetic intoxicant
to again return to
the nagging void

SUMMER SUMMARY

I once knew
all about
the morning
I mean I sensed
it was something special
and in the afternoon
I would run in the sun
evenings I would
romance the prettiest girl
in school
and at night
I would sneak out
under the stars
and ride in cars
wishing I could
get in bars
now I spend all
my time
creating paragraphs
paraphrasing
what can essentially
be broken down
into one word
that I will
now sing:
"amazing!"

SHOPPING AROUND

I wish I was
made by eternity
and that my feet
walked on clouds
defying gravity
and that my eyes
shot laser beams
like a superhero
in a blockbuster
and that my words
were not all bluster
and that I could muster
the prowess to capture
the attention and affection
of the Goddess at the produce
department and that together
we could sire
from our desire
half a dozen babies
but I am only
fooling myself
as I caress the lettuce
pretending it is us
and it is depressing
that for me she will
never be undressing
instead, I will
brood like Brutus
eating salad
with Caesar dressing

DUSTY DUSK

These days
I often melt into
the arms of chairs
and I find myself
gripping the banister
as I head down the stairs
and I prefer
to have guests
visit my thoughts
rather than actually
having them here
and I am selfish
with moments and often
search under furniture
to see if happier times
like my long-lost dog
might be hiding
somewhere
and I was going
to keep these
dark musings
to myself
but after
careful, tearful
consideration
decided
to share

Auto-Reply

If there is a moral
or a meaning
or a coda
or a Yoda
or an epilogue
or a subliminal message
or a higher force
or extra-terrestrials
or additional dimensions
or a way to have instant
replays in slow motion
incorporated into
any given moment
which went by too soon
or some way to get to Tibet
without having to invest in
an expensive air ticket,
or a way to superimpose
myself into the figure
of Michelangelo's Adam
and touch the finger of God
or some way to not fall
in love at first sight
at least twenty times
a day just riding
the New York City Subway

or a way that I could
mend the frayed, fragile
wiring of certain strained
friendships
not to mention a
possibility of striking
out the bloody world conflicts
which escalate
like an Escher
stairway to hell
then let me know
I look forward
to your response
be it snail mail
e-mail
text
or a viral video
answer projected
across the big
Blu-ray sky

The Thanks I Get

Don't suck up
to experience
or flatter reality
or put events
up on a pedestal
because praise
will not raise
your frequency
take it from me
I once exclaimed
to a glorious afternoon
what I thought
of her celestial light
and it didn't stop
the oncoming darkness
of a restless, sleepless night

ANGELIC VISIT

You bring a smile
with you just in case
somebody forgot theirs
and I have seen you
give free rides
to bad moods
and let them off
in a better place
that really cares
and you sneak
into dreams and
act like it is just
some happy
surreal accident
and just yesterday
you promised someone
that tomorrow
would be better
and backed it up
with fair weather
and I remember
you stole my heart
just for fun
but at least you
returned it
when you
were done

FAINT PRAISE

I walked away
from the conversation
about the weather
to stand under the
blue-eyed sky
with its puffy
cloud cheeks
and then I hugged
the trunk of a tree
and asked a squirrel
why we were both
in such a scurry
then I returned inside
the convention
in commemoration
of some man's comb-over
compensation for being
pudgy in all the right
literary places
and though I felt
claustrophobic and bored
there was no escaping
it was me
they were honoring
with this award

INSTRUCTIONS

Encircle me
in a square room
draw a heart
with your lipstick
on the invisible walls
of this out-patient
asylum called
being single
renew my faith
in the subjective error
of consensual
objectivization
then whisper something
politically incorrect
while we privately protest
our right to believe
in that conspiracy theory
about "our" song
and then let's run
barefoot across
green fields
of red grapes
before heartbreak
figures out our
heartbeat algorithm

YOUR ATTENTION PLEASE

While I am talking
everyone is waiting
for their chance
to speak
or the moment to
take their leave
unless I draw them in
with a hook, line, and sinker
they sit there like
Rodin's Thinker
unless I make them laugh
they raise their necks
and look over my shoulder
like craning giraffes
and if the subject
does not concern them
they feign a smile
and say "uh huh"
and that they
better "get goin'"
in fact, I have no
way of knowing
if you even got
to the end
of this poem

ROLEPLAY

When the last person
leaves the room which
had just been filled
with hard liquor
and soft music
bad jokes and
good hugs
I am left
wishing I had told
a certain someone
that this life of the party
is just a fire
running on fumes
and I'd much rather
live in a rom-com
than looney tunes
hoping that if I confess
I will go from
character actor
to love interest

ON SECOND THOUGHT

If and when
I become less ambivalent
about what I might
and might not have meant
then I promise
an official statement
of one hundred percent
decisiveness
and zero divisiveness
will be seen scurrying
out the building
caught on tape by
surveillance
instead, I will surrender
my concealed weapon
of confused confession
and everything can
and will be used against me
like a great inquisition
about yet another moment
of pitiful indecision

Stand Corrected

I scratched my head
rubbed my belly
walked and chewed gum
threw a peace sign
then flipped the bird
winked
raised one eyebrow
danced a jig
crossed my arms
jutted my jaw
thrusted my pelvis
crossed my eyes
knelt down and prayed
stuck out my tongue
followed by a scream
and a whisper
until I shut my mouth
held my breath
sucked in my gut
tiptoed
hemmed and hawed
all because I felt
chastised and
cut down to size
when I was
constructively
criticized

ATTACK OF THE MEGALOMANIAC

I don't know jack
about my ancestors
nor do I give a darn
about my forefathers
and I really should show
more emotion
for the fate of the ocean
but I am too busy
protesting on behalf
of the only
endangered
species that matters
me...
See,
hunters
are poaching
those that blow their
own horns
and these
confidence killers
take the rawhide
of raw talent

and exploit it
in the flea market
of free spirits
where it is sold
to those who hate
everything about
themselves
and then whatever
is left is ground
into stardust
glitter litter
swept away
and then washed
down by suds
of green envy

WISE WORDS

Mr. Richards sat me down
and told me everything
would be alright
and he advised me
to enjoy what is fleeting
while it lasts
and he said,
one day I would be
big and tall
and that I might
not necessarily
have it all
but never to regret
a single thing
that didn't go as planned
and that sometimes you
sit and cry
and at other times
you accept what
you cannot stand
and then he said
all good things
and all bad
come to an end
and then he just poof
disappeared
because Mr. Richards
was my childhood
imaginary friend

Simply Said

I don't know how I do it
I am able to walk and talk
and see Jane run
while also chewing gum
and then I hum
the national anthem
to the heartbeat
of my own drum
you know the one...
that keeps me
above ground
yet still under
the wonder
of the sun...
I am that guy
with his dog
grappling with a past
and a shoelace
in a knot
that cannot
be undone

Waxing Philosophical Legs

Time does not march on
it sneaks out the back door
to have a smoke
its tobacco is what's what
and who you know
its nicotine is
your addiction to meaning
and it is killing you
so you really should stop
driving yourself crazy
worrying about how
you just lost another
twenty-four-hour friend
and instead concentrate on making
peace with your poor concentration
and rich imagination
and take the good with the bad
mix it with the tolerable
and when life
gives you lemons
remember that in the infinite
a pucker is born
every minute

SWINGER'S VOTE

First you tuck in
your gut feelings
then you button up
your slightly wrinkled
emotions
and zip-up
your fly-by-night
preconceptions
about how today
is going to respond
to your casual clothing
which conceals
your naked
position on
political parties
where people pop
other people's
hot air balloons
making your heart
feel like an empty ballot
in the North polling booth
on "no direction day"

KARMICALLY IN DEBT

Let me know when the good part starts
in the meantime, I will be sleepwalking
relying on my auto drive options
and going through the emotions
on a strictly as-needed basis
so please pinch me when it happens
so I won't miss the crescendo
that will sing out with embarrassingly
naked honesty
rather than the retro-rhetoric
of a demigod
who demographically targets
their innuendo
so it hits the diabetic
sweet spot
because I am a critic sick from
metastatic sarcastic cynicism
who is above advice
and won't take criticism
you can't teach this old dog
the new matrix
so if I ain't spiritually broke yet
I don't need a fix

UNJUST BECAUSE

I thought you would be
some sort of lifesaver
thrown out to me
the man over-bored
with his life
but instead, you
gave me
the it's not you
it's me
explanation
which turned out to be
the dickens
to my great expectations
and now I have to struggle
to get through the sluggish
part of this insufferable
nonfiction
book of days
of my life
filled with fastidious detail
like that sudden summer
emotional thunder shower
when words failed
mother nature
all of this leading to
the inevitable Chapter Twelve
at the eleventh hour

Cloud Bursting Your Bubble

I am unable to set the table
and the chairs of my affairs
in place
without attracting lightning
like a fork at a picnic
in a storm
which came shortly
after being warned
and so, I am soaked
to the bone
like a skeleton holding
a collapsed umbrella
a quick cartoon
courtroom sketch
of a defendant
who is all wet
prosecuting himself
in private
and then exonerating
himself in front of a jury
of my puritain peers
who are really just
people in a hurry
to get home
and attend to their own
the bottom line is...
we all think we are all that
but the truth is
nobody really cares

EMPTY NEST

You promised
that it would all
come full circle
for me
like a cast
or class reunion
and I would do
a victory lap
around the lap
of luxury
and you said
I would look
around to see
loved ones
surround me
dancing round
and round
like a marching band
not like this accusatory
Custer's last stand
because blame is
the only thing being
passed from hand to hand
and now nobody's buying
the family brand,
and to think Yoko
didn't even break
up this band

I LOVE NEW YORK

Do not
fall
in love with this city
its jungle of squares
the curves of walking women
swimming up streams of men
Do not become infatuated
with the magic fog
rising from the concrete night
and the sea life symphony
of traffic and psychological pollution
Do not let
yourself succumb
to hypnotic reds
and blues
of broken-hearted Broadway
because this town will never
return your sentiment
you cannot sleep
in the arms of a twenty-four-hour coffee shop
you cannot tiptoe
to kiss the big lips
of billboards
a cabby
can only be your ten-buck
psychologist for the short ride

The fleet of high heels,
hands, hopes and frustration
will never truly be
your family
when you lose even your
darkest powers
they just have to
get to where they are going
I tell you
the city cannot gratify your
greed in the bedroom
Miss Liberty
is only green copper
on a river
and at night
when you close your eyes
she never
sleeps
she is seeing other men
millions of them

LATIN LOVER

Like nails scratching
on a chalkboard
your words create
a dissonant chord
an atonal anomaly
since most of the time
you are sweet to me
now I see your split
personality
and to think
I thought
being with you
would be like
coming in
from the rain
now, I see
that happiness
happens mainly
in Spain

NEST EGG

I should have saved
some moments
in a piggy bank
along with quarters
dimes and nickels
because even a
penny's worth
of yesterday's laughter
would now surely be
worth a million dollars
in the current currency
of curling up in
an easy chair
feeling sorry for
myself for having spent
life without saving up
for a rainy day
like this one
when it seems
I can only
afford a dollar
and a nostalgic
dream

PET PEEVE

The last time
I reached
out to someone
special
I got bit by
their dogmatism
which chased my
romantic ideals
around the room
nipping me
in the bud
of my rosy
outlook
and then
whatever was left
of my raw emotion
was fed to the
cat and mouse
futility of it all
so I will
never show
my true
affection
at my lover's
place
unless she
first
gets her
bullmastiff
out of my face

AND THE WINNER IS...

I presented her
with a private award
for best
certain someone
in my life
and she humbly
accepted my
trivial tribute
made of
secret votes
cast by me
and only
I was there
when she held
the trophy
shaped like a rose
and made of chocolate
then she
tearfully thanked
the amorous powers
that be
for casting her
in the role
of lover
in this stripped-down
off-Broadway
production
in the red
which consists
entirely
of two unknowns
and a bed

LOGIN ATTEMPT

How do you manage
your unruly hair
and your green eyes
all at once
I mean are your
freckles really
hieroglyphics?
because I read
your face like
obscure non-fiction
and skip to the part
that describes your lips
which have set sail
a thousand shipments
of online impulse buys
and I wish I knew
your password
but I have been blocked
after far too many tries

SUGAR DADDY

I should have
set aside a sunny day
for a rainy one
instead, I went broke
on spending sprees
buying presents
for women who
weren't always
present for me
and now
I can't afford
the best things
which come in
tiny packages
yet I still enjoy
window shopping
even if I never go in
I can still wink at
the pretty mannequin

Quantum Leapfrog

They say it is
now possible
to do what
just a few years ago
would have seemed
fantastic
and I have heard about
major breakthroughs
that would boggle
those who grew up
before any of this
was even a glimmer
in the global mind's eye
and pretty soon they are
going to come up with
solutions to problems
that we waste our time
grappling with
when all we have to do is
wait for the experts
to stop teasing
and start revealing
their brand-new body
of evidence
so that
eventually
the unbelievable
becomes commonplace
and taken for granted
like a miracle
on 34th Street

NOTE FOR NOTE

When the snow
the sun and the sea
were like my
wind-blown hair
just another thing
out there within grasp
like the first gasp
of learning to ask
for what should
be a given
like a for goodness
namesake
no need to be stolen
because it is
waiting for you to take
advantage of the newness
the red white and blueness
me the prince
and she the princess
of darkness and lightness
and yes, this may all sound
merely musical
like Sir Lancelot
singing "Camelot"
feeling weak
while acting strong
you see I sold
my whole life
for a song

THE LAST HURRAH

One sweet evening
the many and varied
characters
and caricatures
that I have known
from the sublime
to the incredulous
will attend a
costume ball
that I will throw
where everyone
will be required
to dress
as themselves
and wear the mask
that they are
and we will dance
to the sound of
things
that we have said
to each other
all these years
set against the
techno beat
of now

and we will
work out
our differences
by drinking the
same punch
laced with
grace
and
my "members only"
menagerie of
mankind
and
womankind
will catch up
on old times
as new time
leaves early
to relieve
the babysitter
of tomorrow

PHANTOM OF THE PHANTASM

From crystal clear
to out-of-focus
my vision is
mostly hocus-pocus
from my dream
of spotting my
perfect Pocahontas
in the New York
metropolis
to my over-abundance
of inner reflection
sparkling in my iris
like guilty pleasure
deflection
I am just overly
desirous
like a pre-histrionic
Tyrannosaurus
crushing
every beautiful thing
in this enchanted forest
a long-in-the-tooth
literary sorcerer's apprentice
who learned how
to begin but not
how to end
this overflowing
life and death
sentence

SPECIAL DELIVERY

I am going to think
outside the box
by shipping them
UPS ground
and tracking
their journey
towards that
ultimate destination
which is right
back here
at my home address
where they belong
and I will unpack
them and if there
are still no solutions
my first
knee-jerk reflex
will be
to blame the fact
that I should
have sent them FedEx

GOLDEN CHILD

All the many versions
of me blend together
into an amalgamation
a personality algorithm
set against my heartbeat's
polyrhythm which pumps
raw unbridled energy
throughout my solar
nervous system
making me frenetic, kinetic,
magnetic and just the sort of
manic charismatic
who chews the scenery
and bows to nobody
but those who applaud
for my poetic message
inherent within
my literary inheritance
which I spend
to the credit card max
like a trust fund baby
at Saks

STORYTIME

Don't worry I won't
let go of everything
from the summer
grapes of Bacchus
to the winter storm watch
of a January love affair
or the warm hands
of a telling look
in fact, I am
taking it all in
from the sights
and the in-the-round
sounds of modern
Shakespeare
written within
the daily dialect of
average, everyday
night owls who
hoot and holler
while drinking spirits
and shunning spirituality
in exchange for sensuality
what I am saying is
I see free verse
in the prose
of the universe
and I know there is
no reversal
because this is all
happening live
with no rehearsal
and this possibly
meaningless
structureless plot
is all we've got

BOHO HONEY

I like quirky individuals
of the female persuasion
who wear Diane Keaton hats
sport funky boots
have dimple indentations
shoulders inked with tats
and who own
black cats
and a vintage vinyl
record player
where you can hear
the needle scratch,
I consider them
with their hoop earrings
and smoky mascara
to be the best catch
because they can
adore Plath
yet still know
how to laugh
at an offhand remark
and they often
show great originality
as well as ingenuity
when we are
naked in the dark

CITY SLICKER

My best laid plans
may never get laid
out on the rose
covered bed
in the penthouse suite
where I consummate
victory
over the low
hum
of the huddled
masses
down below
where the hustlers
scam the man
and women
turn to
tricks of the
skin trade
by selling their
souls to the
nine-to-five
grind
and you will
find me there
in the thick
and thin
of things
wishing I could
pull some strings
so that I could
dance
cheek to cheek
instead of
living from
bounced
check to check

DATING DESTINY

I knew as soon as we met
that you were inconsequential
to my sustenance
and existentially irrelevant
to my existence
and yet talking with you
over burgers made me think
of the murmurs of monks
and the untouched buns of nuns
oops maybe I should not have
said such a thing
but our conversation was so nothing
and everything
that it made me think
of the God
of petty pretty things
and how in you
he or she created
a real head-turner
as well as a scalp-scratcher
and I wonder if you
are just like
that sex joke you told
that I will never get
because I was distracted
by how your lip gloss
reflected the sunset

ADULTING

I am going
to stop being
so bull-headed
strong-willed
and stubborn
as a Grinch
who doesn't
like spinach
and I won't
inwardly
stomp my feet
or huff and puff
at the little
defeats that
trip me up
yet, why
don't they
ever tell you
when yuck
sticks to your craw
like Elmer's glue
that big boys don't cry
but grown men do

Spoon and Swoon

Nobody could
top your
abilities
when it came to
making a guy
like me feel
like the world
of your skin
was my oyster
and the sky
of your eyes
my limit
you taught me
the ins and outs of
belly buttons
the highs and lows
of an on-and-off
relationship
your particular
expertise was
the burlesque
tease

of infectious
laughter at all the
wrong places during
a bad movie
and your tearful
confessions at
all the right parts
of a heart-to-heart
you are
a legend
in my mind
as I burn my
soul
walking on
that Hollywood
walk of old flames

DEEP ADVICE

You have
options
you can sigh
and give up
on the why
and just get on
with the how
and you know
live in the now
or you can
bang your head
against the wall
between you
and having it all
in any case
love will never
find ya
if you spend all
your time
digging a hole
to China

Spine Shiver

The autumn wind
speaks to me
of love that once ran
wicked through the streets
wild and alive
feeding off MSG
in Chinatown
and tequila in dive bars
on Ludlow
when the biggest sin of all
was rolling out of bed at noon
and brunching till three
on Columbus Avenue NYC
and November knows
so much about sexy sweaters
worn by graduate students
who swoon like textbook cases
of Ivy League psychosis
and I don't know if you know
but the longer I live
the less I am able to recall
the simple thrill
of a midnight phone call
in a railroad apartment
from a sobbing
Balanchine ballerina
who claimed
I misunderstood
her barefoot dance
on the cold Sandalwood

AFTERGLOW

Last night
changed everything
and nothing
because it wasn't
like we climbed Everest
but it did feel like
we stopped time
yet morning came
like it always does
a real buzzkill
where you scrambled
for your clothing
and your composure
and we are both adults
so no real need
for closure
and then I closed
the door
and you were gone
yet I noticed that
all the lights in
the house
and my six senses
were still
turned on

FIRST IMPRESSION

You only know
a spec of my cosmos
and that is because
you focus
on the good side
of my photogenic
personality
but I truly come to life only
behind the scenes
in the secret-keeping alleys
or the closed-door meeting
between my internal introverts
and extroverts
who pervert goodness
and promote madness
in the push and pull
happy sadness
that gives way
to the shrouded things
I do and say,
anyway, I hope
my quirky, quivering
eager beaver smile
doesn't scare you away

LOVE ABUSE

You are unkind
and beautiful
and your temper
tantrums
rattle the walls
yet you are the
seventh thing
I wonder about
the world
the first six
don't even matter
if they don't include
the pyramid mystery
of your closed eyes
when you
finally sleep
after having
said something
off-the-cuff
off-the-rails
of the Richter scale
that cuts deep
leaving me
forever counting
slaughtered sheep

Opposites Attract

Whether it is
a dream
or a nightmare
only matters if it
happens while you
are awake or sleeping
and if you don't know
then it could mean
you are stuck between
life and death
or torn between
darkness and light
or grappling with
good and bad
in any case
personally, I prefer
you happy
rather than sad
because you
are the most
perfect
personification
of yin and yang
I have ever had

ARTS AND CRAFTS

I carve into life
I paint and patina
over time
and journal on
the white pages
of personal space
I then speak
over sound
as if in a lover's
quarrel with every
intention of making up
with the magnetic
solar powers of
the six dimensions
and the seven seas
coupled with
the birds and the bees
and knowing my
self-value on
the marketplace
of the human race
it is no wonder
I say, "bless me"
whenever I sneeze

GRACEFUL EXIT

When you
changed
your mind
I noticed a chill
in the air
and heartbreak
went bump
in the night
and I wondered
about strangers
above on
night flights
headed to
non-disclosed
destinations
I even thought
about
presidential
resignations
and never
to be used
dinner reservations
or a really sad
happy hour
at a dive bar
anyway, I still
would be honored
to escort you
to your car

ABOUT THE AUTHOR

Ivan Jenson is a fine artist, novelist and popular contemporary poet who lives in Grand Rapids, Michigan. His artwork was featured in Art in America, Art News, and *Interview Magazine* and has sold at auction at Christie's.

Amongst Ivan's commissions are the final portrait of the late Malcolm Forbes and a painting titled "Absolut Jenson" for Absolut Vodka's national ad campaign. His Absolut paintings are in the collec- tion of the Spritmuseum, the museum of spirits in Stockholm, Sweden. Jenson's painting of the "Marlboro Man" was collected by the Philip Morris corporation.

His novels, *Dead Artist* and *Seeing Soriah*, illustrate the creative, often dramatic lives of artists. Jenson's poetry is widely published (with over 100 poems published in the US, UK and Europe) in a variety of literary media. He has published a poetry book, *Media Child and Other Poems*, and two novels, *Marketing Mia* and *Erotic Rights*.

Mundane Miracles hit number 1 on Amazon in American Poetry. **www.ivanjenson.com**

ABOUT
CITY STONE PUBLISHING

*A publisher with a passion for the written word
and a heart that beats for indie authors*

We are an imaginative and enthusiastic indie publisher.

Our ambition is twofold:
To develop outstanding books and work alongside our authors.
To be a beacon of advice and a provider of services for indie authors.

We are not just about the books; we build relationships with our
authors. Because we both write, we know what (indie) authors want.
That is how we work: in cooperation and partnership with our
authors.

From dark and gritty crime thrillers, adventurous fantasy, entertaining
women's fiction, and intriguing contemporary novels to interesting
and insightful non-fiction and visionary poetry, we publish it all.

Visit our website: **www.citystonepublishing.com**

Made in the USA
Monee, IL
28 July 2023